For The Journey

A Year On The Cuckmere Pilgrim Path

Kevin Scully

Poet In Residence
Cuckmere Pilgrim Path
2022 - 2023

Published by St Michael and All Angels, Berwick. 2023

Copyright © Kevin Scully 2023
All rights reserved

Author's website
www.kevin-scully.com

Kevin Scully has asserted his right under
the Copyright, designs and Patents Act 1988
to be identified as the author of this work

ISBN 978-0-9553859-1-9

CONTENTS

Pilgrim 1

For The Journey 2

The other side of the arch 3

Three bells. 4

It's Cuckmere 5

Shall the potter be regarded as the clay? 6

They will stamp 7

Through a glass darkly 8

In Arlington Churchyard 9

Cuckmere conundrum 10

Man Up In Wilmington 11

The Good Shepherd, Lullington 12

Uphill from The Tye 13

The economics of a miracle worker. 14

The Score 15

Cuckmere Koan 16

One last climb. 17

Notes on the poems. 18

Pilgrim

do not
          start here
you can not
          start here
you must start
          where you are
or rather
          where you were
at the start

do not
          start now
do not
          even try

your journey
          started
                    long before

FOR THE JOURNEY

We are advised to travel light. One pack,
clothes that fold, can be layered, pressed down.
Washable, two of each, or better, one to be hung
to dry overnight. Stout boots, a broad brimmed hat,
protection against the sun, creams to comfort
bites and stings. Just the necessary for hygiene;
no warpaint—that hides our true faces.

But there is this other bag, the one we fill with things
we cannot see: all the regrets, resentments and recriminations
done by or to us. They slip invisibly onto our back
yet are weighty as we plod along solo or in company,
looking for that cliff, well or body of water
where we can cast it to its death and each
new step springs into a jeté.

The other side of the arch

Every church conceals something.
When Bloomsbury bloomed
in Berwick, some paintings
were missing to faithful eyes.
The sanctuary is yours now:
                    step up.

When they moved the altar
the priest numbered them:
five aside, wise and foolish.
Virgins with his back to that place,
bridesmaids modernly face to face:
                    look up.

Holman Hunt-like the door opens
from within, a glimmer crack
of hope falls askance. Dozing,
alert, sheep, goat, bright, dim,
the cry rings out:
                    Here comes the groom.

Three bells

i

There is no method here.
In Singapore, pass votive gifts
to mount stairs to increasing

stillness of displays until you
reach a relic—
a tooth of the Buddha.

Last floor from the sky
is a garden with a tower and
a bell to toll a prayer.

ii

You take a pletna
over Lake Bled
for engineless access

onto an island,
a perfect setting
for contemplation

until you pull a rope
to sound your wish.
Done three times,

according to some Pope,
it will come true.

iii

No such promise here,
in earthbound Alciston.

Shaped to contain
the bell invites you:

strike me and I will
resonate for you.

It's Cuckmere
as in cuckoo.
Not Cuckmere
as in duck.

There could have been
other rhymes, but I think
the ornithological will do.

Shall the potter be regarded as the clay?
for Jonathan Chiswell Jones

If God has no hands but ours,
as Teresa of Avila is said to have said,
and the magisterial being is solely
spirit, whose breath was blown
into Adam's nostrils?

    And when Paul asks
Has the potter no right over the clay?
are we right to proclaim ourselves
the end in all things?

    Yet, Jonathan, you dug earth,
turned the wheel, fired the kiln, placed pots
in alcoves, suggesting we leave messages,
walk with them along the path.

I take the lid off one and, as prayers
rumble out, read the messages:
thanksgiving; rejoicing; in memory;
lamenting; delighting; beseeching;
God help me; There be witches here.

    You made your creation
a receptacle, like the questionable God and
the universe.

        There is no silence here.

They will stamp
your passport if you have one.
Symbols mirror the still flight of cock,
fish (is it a shark?) flèches (flaming bell/angel?) cross to advertise the
one revealed upon it. And how are the patrons—Peter, Mary, Good Shepherd,
Michael and his crew, Pancras and Andrew (motley bunch)—applied
to windicators that point the way,
but maybe it's not to the one
you are trudging.

Through a glass darkly, Selmeston
for Léonie Seliger

This window works in reverse:
it lights through our translucent lives
like gradient marks on a walker's map.

Defined colours somehow bleed into shades
of doubtful complexion: stridency in blue
splatters into harvest gold, stripling
green, martyrs' blood red, scurry-cloud
grey, fingerprint black in a hidden cross.

As we strike out from this dark sanctum,
we encounter a sky that buries us in the earth
beneath our pilgrim booted feet.

In Arlington Churchyard

As kids we burnt the edges of old paper:
crushed, abused and buried,
these were our hallmarks of antiquity.
We offered occluded clues to
treasure, precious and always somewhere
                            under the ground

Our ancestors struggled, as we do,
with what to do with the dead: barrows,
mounds, tombs and wayside gifts,
all weighted with words from the sublime
to the mawkish. Unrestrained, untrained but
                            from the heart

Trowel handlers on digs surprise
themselves with villages, diverse and complex,
landfill alongside hoards of gold and silver.
Waste and wonder are earthly companions
but sometimes it's just stuff. We want it
                            out of sight

Some stones fade, others were never
built to hold scratchings from the present
to the future of a past, timeless as we look
                            earth to earth

Cuckmere conundrum

I have no idea
where I am
but
I can always
go back the way
I came.

MAN UP IN WILMINGTON

The Giant keeps his secret and from his hillside
flings out a perpetual challenge—The Revd A. A. Evans

It was over the head of Long Man,
three of us speaking about the destruction
of Europe through a referendum.
We polished our Eurodentials
to defy the fearful lurching
to political starboard.

Red, white, blue, whatever way,
didn't help the man we could not see,
whose head was under our backsides.
He too has had a colourful life—
camouflage green in war, yellow brick,
now whited concrete blocks to stand out.

And even he has had to adapt,
what with the removal of his public
parts so offensive to Victorians,
but still he stands ready
with his walking poles or javelins
daring walkers below

but lost from above.

THE GOOD SHEPHERD
Lullington

Hunted, survivor, outlier,
rebel, ruin, relic,
smallest in your county
but grand as a cathedral,
prayer blows in and out
of doors and windows
like the dust and aching
limbs of walkers taking
       refuge.

Uphill from The Tye

So much begins and ends here: The National Trust
(a Clergy House with no priests in evidence)
Steamer Trading (a flash in more than pans),
records from old times, no longer spinning
in vinyl or plastic. There are survivors—pubs,
cafés, boutiques, a bookshop named after
The Bard of another river, Avon, not Cuckmere.

Once, in the wide naved church, I watch a friend
commit another friend to eternity; later, we drank
to the gentle man's memory at his expense, one more
gesture of hospitality, typical of his life. Respect
was reflected in the number of mourners, so many
this service shifted from the village church he had served
so long. So we came here, where so much begins and ends.

The economics of a miracle worker

This corner of an English field lies forever
Elijah: a path between crops of potential,
rapeseed (not quite the exile's olives)
and wheat, crushed and milled into more than
staples of life; but with power to sustain
economies for a widow and her son,
gifts which not only sustain; they sell.

Can a prophet's mantle drop here in Sussex?
Is there a disciple who walks these ways,
clothes rent, and looks Elisha-like into the sky,
seeing over the Downs fiery chariots drawn by
flaming horses for more than bread and oil and coin?

THE SCORE
Twenty years of Blee

The vicar is in court again.
His crime? Moving furniture.
Yet there is so much more
we could convict him of:

he points to the sky
to God, but through a bird,
whose name he knows
in Latin and English;

sees connections in landscape,
draws contours in faith,
makes molehill mysteries
out of the commonplace;

preaches to people dulled
by creativity of metaphor,
calling on language to be
the invention of excuses;

encourages the bespoke for
memorials for those to be buried
in confines of yards on edge
of pasture and cultivation.

And worse still, in all this,
he listens and prays as he looks
at widening skies, pondering
possibilities up the Downs

Cuckmere Koan

             The trouble is,
in circles.   he said,
  goes around   a pilgrim starts
he said,   in one place,
  But this one   or even many,
    a castle, a house.   but ends somewhere:
       a shrine, a temple,

One last climb

There's a glimpse of sea—I know, I have seen it
once or twice—when you lean into the wind
at the top. Getting there takes an effort. I leave
the designated path and its shell-emblazoned
signposts to take a short, sharp, pull up the track
which, despite my age, still has the romance
of smugglers carting contraband into the village below.

I stumble, my boot's downworn heel
wobbles me, feel sockdamp, look and notice
growing cracks behind the toecap,
a fraying lace. Signs enough, as though
my puffing chest and pumping heart were not,
to pause, sit down and wait. The view will still
be there. I know it will. I have seen it before.

Notes on the poems:

The other side of the arch
Quentin Bell's 1942 painting of 'The Wise And Foolish Bridesmaids' cannot be seen from the nave of Berwick Church, as it is hidden on the rear of the chancel arch. It is based on the parable of Jesus Matthew Ch.25 v.1-4. It is best viewed from the chancel of the church.

Three Bells
is a response to the Pilgrim Bell in Alciston Church donated by the churchwarden, Michele Boys. It was commissioned for the Cuckmere Pilgrim Path and made at Whitechapel Bell Foundry in 2021. Walkers are invited to strike the bell and listen to the sound. This is an acoustic alternative to lighting a candle. In the bell tower are two bells dating back to c. 1380.

Shall The Potter
The ceramicist Jonathan Chiswell Jones (www.jcjpottery.co.uk) made seven pots. Clay was harvested from a field near Arlington along the Cuckmere Pilgrim Path in the vicinity of a roman brick works. In each church there is a pot into which walkers are invited to place something—a reflection, poem, observation or prayer—for others to discover.

They will stamp
A card is available for walkers to take with them and stamp at each church with an image of the weather vane of that church —hence the flèche shape of the poem. This card can be sent to a friend with a message written on the back. For example, the walk can be undertaken as an act of prayer or reflection for someone else, as they carry them in their thoughts and prayers along the path.

The Pilgrim Window
in Selmeston Church was designed and made by Léonie Seliger at the Canterbury Studios to celebrate the Cuckmere Pilgrim Path. It was installed in 2022 in memory of June Mockett. A pamphlet describing the window is available in the church.

Man Up In Wilmington
The brick outline of the Long Man on the escarpment of Windover Hill at Wilmington dates back to the 1550's. There are many theories about the figure. This poem joins the plethora of responses that have been made, with greater and lesser accuracy, to this iconic landmark.

The Good Shepherd, Lullington
Claimed to be the smallest church in England, it is the surviving chancel of a larger church and sits in a stunning location on the side of the Downs.

Uphill From The Tye
The Tye is the green in the centre of Alfriston outside the church. The Clergy House was bought for £10 by the newly formed National Trust in 1896 and became its initial project. The first branch of the successful kitchenware chain, Steamer Trading was opened in 1985 by Liz and David Phillips and grew into a chain of stores. The shop closed in 2017 and the brand was subsumed by a different chain.

The Score
The Revd Peter Blee celebrated 20 years as priest to five Sussex churches 2023. Restoration of the Berwick Church paintings in 2021 included a proposal to remove Victorian and 1970s pews. The process was arduous, involved two Consistory Court hearings, held in the church, and an appeal to the Court of Arches. Kevin attended the final hearing in the church at which Peter and others gave evidence.

Cuckmere Koan
The poem plays on the circularity of the Cuckmere Pilgrim Path which begins and ends at St Andrew's, Alfriston.

One Last Climb
There are number of tracks up to the South Downs. One ascends to the top of Windover Hill above the Long Man. From the top of the hill is a magnificent view which includes the English Channel. Some paths on the escarpment are in cuttings which are said to have provided cover for smugglers bringing in contraband from the coast.